HANDWRITING PRACTICE 2ND GRADE

CHILDREN'S READING & WRITING EDUCATION BOOKS

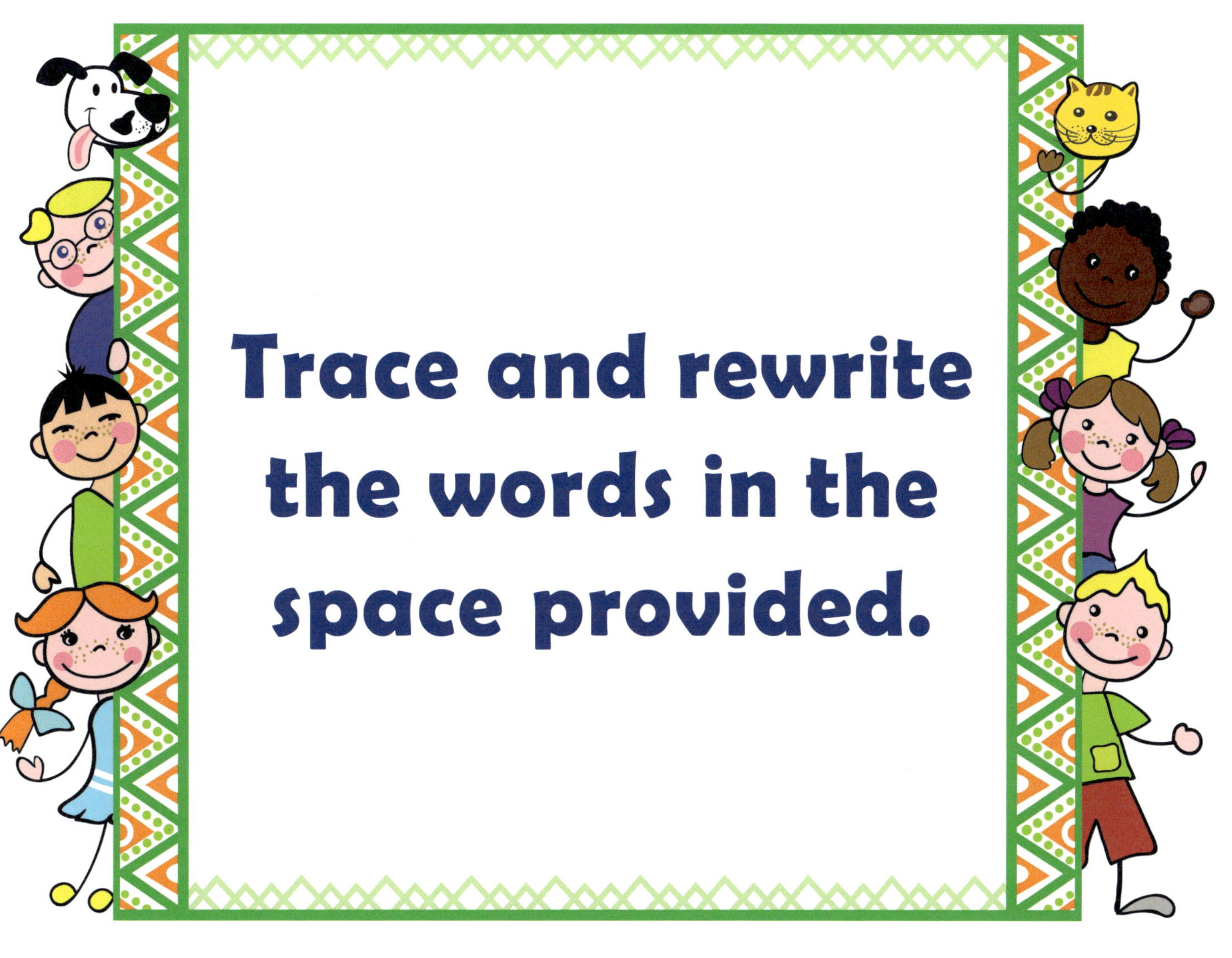

Trace and rewrite the words in the space provided.

agree   *agree*

arrive   *arrive*

atlas

atlas

award

award

aware
aware
banner
banner

beach   *beach*

board   *board*

bounce *bounce*

career *career*

connect
connect
collect
collect

couple couple

curious curious

demolish

demolish

discard

discard

doubt   *doubt*

dozen   *dozen*

enemy

enemy

evening

evening

excess
excess
famous
famous

finally

finally

frighten

frighten

fuel *fuel*

gravity *gravity*

greedy   *greedy*

harm   *harm*

herd   *herd*

idea   *idea*

insect
insect

invent
invent

island

island

leader

leader

lizard

lizard

leap

leap

local

local

luxury

luxury

mention   *mention*

motor   *motor*

nervous
nervous
nibble
nibble

notice
notice
ocean
ocean

pack *pack*

pale *pale*

parade   *parade*

peak   *peak*

planet   *planet*

present   *present*

reflect   *reflect*

rumor   *rumor*

scholar scholar

search search

settle
settle
share
share

shelter
shelter
shiver
shiver

slight   *slight*

smooth   *smooth*

steady *steady*

support *support*

telescope telescope

tremble tremble

universe
universe
village
village

wealthy wealthy

weak weak

whisper   *whisper*

wonder   *wonder*

yard

yard

zigzag

zigzag

Made in the USA
Monee, IL
07 July 2026

56551301R00026